Drama for Students, Volume 7

Staff

Editorial: David M. Galens, *Editor*. Tim Akers, Andrea Henry, Mark Milne, and Kathleen Wilson, *Contributing Editors*. James Draper, *Managing Editor*. David Galens and Lynn Koch, *"For Students" Line Coordinators*. Jeffery Chapman, *Programmer/Analyst*.

Research: Victoria B. Cariappa, *Research Manager*. Andrew Guy Malonis, Barbara McNeil, Gary J. Oudersluys, Maureen Richards, and Cheryl L. Warnock, *Research Specialists*. Patricia Tsune Ballard, Wendy K. Festerling, Tamara C. Nott, Tracie A. Richardson, Corrine A. Stocker, and, Robert Whaley, *Research Associates*. Phyllis J. Blackman, Tim Lehnerer, and Patricia L. Love, *Research Assistants*.

Permissions: Maria Franklin, *Permissions Manager*. Kimberly F. Smilay, *Permissions*

Specialist. Kelly A. Quin, *Permissions Associate.* Sandra K. Gore, *Permissions Assistant.*

Graphic Services: Randy Bassett, *Image Database Supervisor.* Robert Duncan and Michael Logusz, *Imaging Specialists.* Pamela A. Reed, *Imaging Coordinator.* Gary Leach, *Macintosh Artist.*

Product Design: Cynthia Baldwin, *Product Design Manager.* Cover Design: Michelle DiMercurio, *Art Director.* Page Design: Pamela A. E. Galbreath, *Senior Art Director.*

Copyright Notice

Since this page cannot legibly accommodate all copyright notices, the acknowledgments constitute an extension of the copyright notice.

While every effort has been made to secure permission to reprint material and to ensure the reliability of the information presented in this publication, the Gale Group neither guarantees the accuracy of the data contained herein nor assumes any responsibility for errors, omissions, or discrepancies. Gale accepts no payment for listing; and inclusion in the publication of any organization, agency, institution, publication, service, or individual does not imply endorsement of the editors or publisher. Errors brought to the attention of the publisher and verified to the satisfaction of the publisher will be corrected in future editions.

This publication is a creative work fully protected by all applicable copyright laws, as well as by misappropriation, trade secret, unfair competition, and other applicable laws. The authors and editors of this work have added value to the underlying factual material herein through one or more of the following: unique and original selection, coordination, expression, arrangement, and classification of information. All rights to this publication will be vigorously defended.

© 2000 Gale Group
27500 Drake Rd.
Farmington Hills, MI 48331-3535

Gale Group and Design is a trademark used herein under license.

All rights reserved including the right of reproduction in whole or in part in any form.

This book is printed on acid-free paper that meets the minimum requirements of American National Standard for Information Sciences—Permanence Paper for Printed Library Materials, ANSI Z39.48-1984.

ISBN 0-7876-4081-6
ISSN 1094-9232
Printed in the United States of America

10 9 8 7 6 5 4

A Taste of Honey

Shelagh Delaney 1958

Introduction

When Shelagh Delaney began working on *A Taste of Honey*, she intended the material to be a novel; but instead, in what has become a very famous story, Delaney became disgusted at the lack of substance found in plays currently being produced for the stage and decided to rework her fledgling novel into a play. It took her two weeks. *A Taste of Honey* opened at the Theatre Royal, Stratford East in London on May 27, 1958. On February 10, 1959, Delaney's play moved to Wyndham's Theatre in London's West End, and on October 4, 1960, the play opened on Broadway at New York City's Lyceum Theatre. Delaney's play opened to mixed reviews. In many cases, her characters were praised for their honest, realistic voices. The play was also singled out for its accurate depictions of working class lives.

Yet there was also concern that too much praise for the play's nineteen-year-old author would make it difficult for her to ever create another hit play, the theory being that early success might prove so intimidating that she could never live up to her first accomplishment. In a sense, this is what happened, since Delaney never wrote another play that achieved the success of *A Taste of Honey*. However, this first play did earn several awards, including the Charles Henry Foyle New Play award in 1958 and the New York Drama Critics Award in 1961. The film version won the British Academy Award for best picture in 1961 and a best supporting actress award for Dora Bryan. The film also won two additional awards at the Cannes Film Festival in 1962 for best actor (Murray Melvin) and best actress (Rita Tushingham). Much of the credit for the play's success is attributed to Joan Littlewood, whose experimental Theatre Workshop first received and produced the play.

Author Biography

Shelagh Delaney was born November 25, 1939, in Salford, Lancashire, England. Her father, a bus inspector, and her mother were part of the English working class, the social group that informs of her writing. Delaney attended Broughton Secondary School but began writing even before she completed her education. She had no further interest in formal education, and after she left school, she held a number of jobs, including salesgirl, usherette, and clerk.

A Taste of Honey was produced when Delaney was eighteen-years-old. Although this play was originally being written as a novel, it was rewritten as a play in response to Delaney's dissatisfaction with contemporary theatre. Delaney felt that she could write a better play, with more realistic dialogue, than the plays that were currently being staged. *A Taste of Honey* became an unexpected hit, winning several awards both as a play and later as a film. Delaney followed with another play, *The Lion in Love*, two years later (1960). She did not write another play for nearly twenty years.

Instead, Delaney focused on short stories, *Sweetly Sings the Donkey* (1963); screenplays, *Charlie Bubbles* (1968) and *The Raging Moon* (1970); and television plays, *Did Your Nanny Come from Bergen?* (1970), *St. Martin's Summer* (1974), and *Find Me First* (1979). In 1979, Delaney again wrote for the theatre when she adapted *The House That Jack Built*, a BBC television script she had written in 1977. Delaney followed this stage work with two radio plays, *So Does the Nightingale* (1980) and *Don't Worry about Matilda* (1981). After another television play, *Rape* (1981), Delaney was asked to write a screenplay based on the true story of a women who was executed for murder. This work became the film *Dance with a Stranger* (1985). Delaney has also contributed articles for the *New York Times Magazine*, the *Saturday Evening Post, Cosmopolitan*, and *Evergreen Review*.

Delaney's first play proved a difficult act to follow, and none of her subsequent work received the same critical acclaim that greeted *A Taste of Honey*, although her collection of short, autobiographical stories, *Sweetly Sings the Donkey*, was considered a critical success. Delaney believes in social protest and has not been afraid to speak out on the need for a more realistic theatre, one that depicts the working class environment of many British citizens. Delaney lives in London, where she was made a fellow of the Royal Society of Literature in 1985.

Plot Summary

Act I, scene i

The act opens with Helen and Jo in the process of moving into their new flat. It is cold, squalid, and damp. Helen is sick with a cold, but not too sick to engage in bickering conversation with her daughter, Jo. The two squabble effortlessly over minor issues, such where the heat is located, making coffee, or even how often to bathe. In the midst of this activity, Helen's boyfriend, Peter, enters. He is much younger than Helen. It becomes clear that Helen has moved to hide from Peter, who is very surprised to learn that Helen has a daughter. Failing to engage the older women in sex, Peter asks Helen to leave with him and get a drink. He also asks her to marry him, but is it unclear if he is actually serious about marriage or simply trying to get Helen to sleep with him. When Helen continues to insist that she is too ill to go out, Peter finally leaves. Helen tells Jo to leave the unpacking, since everything is best hidden in the dark. The scene ends with their exiting to go to bed.

Act I, scene ii

The scene opens on Jo and a young black man. He is walking her to her door and stops to kiss her. He asks her to marry him, and when she realizes he is serious, Jo says yes. The Boy pulls from his pocket a ring, but it is too large for Jo's finger, and so, she places the ring on a ribbon and ties it about her neck. The Boy is in the navy and will soon be leaving for six months at sea. After he leaves to go out with his friends, Helen begins to quiz Jo about why she looks so happy. Jo and Helen begin speaking of Jo's father, and the audience learns that many years earlier, Helen's husband had divorced her because he was not the father of the child (Jo) that Helen was expecting.

Helen tells Jo that she is going to marry Peter. At Jo's shocked exclamation that he is much younger, Helen reminds her daughter that at forty, she is scarcely old and dried up. Peter enters, and the moment Helen leaves to dress, he and Jo begin to argue. When Helen enters again, she tells Jo that Peter has bought a house in which they will live. As soon as Helen leaves again, Jo begins to go through the photos in Peter's wallet, accusing him of having many girlfriends. When Helen enters again, they all begin arguing, and finally Helen and Peter leave, and Jo begins to cry. The Boy enters and begins to sooth Jo. In her loneliness, she invites him to stay with her during the Christmas holidays.

The lights fade down and Helen enters with an assortment of boxes containing her wedding clothes. She finds the ring that The Boy gave Jo and seizes it, complaining that Jo is ruining her life in choosing marriage at such a young age. After Jo asks her, Helen begins to tell Jo about her father, whom Jo learns was an idiot. Jo immediately begins to worry that she has inherited her father's weak mind, and

Helen recounts that Jo was the result of one brief encounter with a man whom she really did not know. The act ends with Helen rushing out to her own wedding.

Act II, scene i

It is summer, about six months later. The scene opens with an obviously pregnant Jo entering with her friend Geof. He has been evicted from his apartment, probably because he is homosexual. He needs a place to stay, and Jo invites him to stay in the apartment. Geof wants to take care of her, and over the coming month, he does just that, cleaning and preparing for the coming baby. Jo is full of emotions, hating the idea of love and motherhood but at the same time needing someone to love her. She calls Geof her big sister, and he is very tolerant of her mood swings. He has also been supporting her, paying the rent and buying food.

Geof very much wants to be a father to Jo's coming child. He is genuinely fond of Jo and is even willing to accept a heterosexual lifestyle if it means he will have a place in Jo's and the baby's future. Goef tries to kiss Jo and asks her to marry him, but she rejects his advances, saying she hates sex. Geof tells Jo that he would sooner be dead than leave her, and they agree that he can stay; they will continue together as they have for the past month. Helen enters. Geof has sent for Helen, reasoning that Jo really needs her mother. But he fails to understand the sordid nature of their relationship.

Helen is angry that Jo is pregnant and tells her that everyone is calling her a whore. After some angry, harsh, and accusatory words are exchanged, Jo threatens to jump out the window if Helen does not leave. In the silence that follows, Jo sends Geof to make coffee, and Helen continues to bully Jo.

Helen tries to leave Jo some money, and just as she is ready to leave, Peter enters. He is as loud and obnoxious as he was six months earlier, and he is drunk and abusive. He begins to berate Helen, saying he married his mother, an old bag, by mistake. A clearly embarrassed Helen tries to silence him, but Peter lets slip that he has been chasing young women. Helen is upset. Peter stumbles and passes out. In a few moments he is back on stage, looking slightly more sober. Peter refuses to allow Helen to bring Jo back to their home, and although Helen hesitates about leaving Jo, she runs out after Peter. As the scene ends, Jo is once again alone with Geof, and Peter has taken the money that Helen intended to leave for Jo.

Act II, scene ii

It is a few months later, and Jo's baby is due any day. Geof is cleaning, as Jo sits watching him. As they begin to talk, it becomes clear that Jo is worried that her child will be like her own father, the village idiot. But Geof tells her that Helen undoubtedly lied about Jo's father. Jo is once again emotional, and when Geof suggests that she begin preparing for the baby, Jo insists she intends to kill it. Geof has made a cake and as they prepare to celebrate the end of his schooling and exams and the coming baby, Helen walks in, loaded with packages. Jo and Helen immediately begin to argue over whether Jo will go to the hospital to have the baby. Jo insists she will have her baby in the apartment.

Helen insults Geof, and he leaves. Jo chastises Helen for being rude to Geof, but she seems not to have noticed. Within moments, Helen is forced to admit that Peter has thrown her out and run off with a younger woman. Jo leaves to go lie down, and Geof enters with a bag of food. Helen is assuming a motherly role, insisting on cleaning and caring for Jo. Although she readily admits that she never remembers Jo when she's with a man, Helen's new single status has reminded her of her daughter and impending grandchild. Even though Jo wants Geof to be with her when the baby comes, Helen has sent him away. Jo finally tells her mother that the baby will be black, and a shocked Helen suggests they drown the child or give it away. The play ends with Helen rushing off stage to find a bar and a drink but promising that she will be back.

Characters

The Boy

The Boy is a black sailor who appears briefly, professing love for Jo. He asks her to marry him and gives her a ring. They spend a week together during Christmas, but then he leaves for a six month tour at sea. The Boy never reappears in Jo's life and does not know that she is carrying his child.

Helen

Helen is described as a semi-whore who drinks too much. As the play opens, she has a cold and has moved herself and daughter into a chilly, squalid flat. Helen is young, barely forty. She has been married and divorced, but her daughter, Jo, is the result of a brief affair with another man. Helen has been involved with many men, and she has not been any kind of real mother to Jo, who appears to desperately need maternal guidance. Helen thinks first and foremost of her own pleasure. She chooses to marry Peter, perhaps because she loves him, but also because he has money to keep her. When Peter finally throws Helen out for a younger woman, she goes back to Jo, suddenly remembering that Jo is her daughter. Jo accuses Helen of never really being a mother to her. And, indeed, it appears that Helen is incapable of thinking of anything except her own needs.

Media Adaptations

A Taste of Honey was adapted as a film in 1961, earning popular success and a number of critical awards. The film stars Rita Tushingham, Robert Stephens, Dora Bryan, Murray Melvin, and Paul Danquah. The director was Tony Richardson, who also adapted the screenplay with Delaney.

Geof

See Geoffrey Ingram

Geoffrey Ingram

Geof is a homosexual art student and friend of Jo's. His landlady has thrown him out on the street, and he begins to care for Jo, sleeping on her couch. Geof genuinely loves Jo. He is perhaps the only person who completely loves and cares for her.

Geof tolerates Jo's emotional outbursts and even tries to reunite her with her mother, but he discovers that Helen is too self-centered to ever love anyone but herself. Geof also offers Jo financial support, paying the rent, buying food, and performing domestic tasks like cleaning and cooking. Although Helen turns up repeatedly, whenever she happens to remember that she has a daughter or needs a place to go, it is Geof who is the steadying influence in Jo's life.

Jimmie

See The Boy

Jo

See Josephine

Josephine

Jo is Helen's daughter. She never knew her real father, but she does know that Helen's husband divorced her after she became pregnant with another man's child. Jo has many questions about her real father, but she is upset to learn that he was probably mentally deficient, an "idiot," according to Helen. Jo is in love with a young black sailor. He arrives to comfort her after Helen leaves to marry Peter. The two spend a few brief days together, and after he has left for a six month tour at sea, Jo discovers that she is pregnant.

Jo has never experienced the love of a mother. She has been repeatedly abandoned by Helen, who did not want a child and has never assumed any responsibility or care for Jo. Jo is not at all sure that she wants the child she is expecting, nor is she sure what she will do with it when it appears. However, by the end of the play, it appears that Jo has rejected her mother's life for the stability that her friendship with Geof offers.

Peter Smith

Peter is about ten years younger than Helen. He fancies himself quite a lady's man, carrying photos of many old girlfriends in his wallet. He drinks too much, as does Helen. Peter is as self-centered as Helen, first begging her to marry him and then chasing other women. Peter is cruel and rude, caring little for anyone's feeling. He treats Jo, the daughter of the woman he professes to love, as a troublesome irritation to be gotten rid of. When Peter throws Helen out, it comes as no surprise to anyone involved.

Themes

Alienation and Loneliness

Jo has essentially been abandoned by her mother. This has been a life-long pattern, but it becomes overwhelming when Helen moves her daughter to a new flat just before Christmas and then leaves almost immediately with her boyfriend. Jo's loneliness directly leads to her pregnancy. When her mother, Helen, leaves with Peter, Jo dissolves into tears. The young black man, who professes to love her, appears, and Jo invites him to stay with her for the Christmas holidays. In the previous scene, Jo is resistant to any intimacy with this young man, who is leaving for a six-month tour at sea with the navy. But when he appears later at her flat, Jo is so overwhelmed with loneliness that she throws away her future plans for work, right along with her inhibitions.

Duty and Responsibility

Helen has a duty to care for her daughter, but she assumes no responsibility for her actions nor does she assume the mother's role. Helen is ready to run off with a man, quite literally, at a moment's notice. She never considers what will happen to her child. And it becomes clear as the play progresses that this has been a frequent occurrence in Jo's life. Helen has never considered her daughter's feelings or assumed any responsibility for her care. Jo is expected to care for herself, and apparently she has done so for some time before the play opens. Helen thinks so little of her child that she never even tells the men with whom she is involved that she has a daughter. This means that Jo has no model for motherhood on which to base her own behavior. This is an issue of the last act when Jo struggles with her impending motherhood and her ambivalence over having a child of her own. There is ample evidence that, with her child, Jo will repeat the cycle of neglect that Helen started.

Friendship

Geof proves his worth as a friend through the efforts he makes to care for Jo. As her only friend, he moves in when she most needs help. Because she does not want anyone to see her, Jo cannot work, and thus, she has no funds with which to pay for rent and food. Geof needs a place to stay, having been evicted because he is homosexual, and Jo offers him her living room couch as a bed. Geof becomes Jo's only friend. He pays the rent and buys and prepares the food. His friendship extends to an attempted reunion between Jo and her mother—though Geof fails to realize the extent of Helen's selfishness. He is the only person who unconditionally loves Jo. Geof offers her loyal, generous friendship, something she has never known and is not quite sure how to accept.

Mother and Daughter Relationship

A central theme in this play is the nature of mother/daughter love. In the case of Helen and Jo, there seems to be no real parent/child relationship in the traditional sense. Helen does not act like a mother, nurturing and caring for her child. Jo does not act like a child, respecting and obeying her parent. In fact, Jo does not address Helen as "mother," preferring to call her by her given name. Jo addresses her mother as "Helen" as a form of disrespect.

Topics for Further Study

- Discuss the interracial love affair between Jo and the character known as The Boy. In view of her mother's reaction at the end of Act II, how much of a factor was race in choosing him as a date and later as a lover?

- Research the economic conditions of working class women in northern England during the twentieth century. What opportunities existed for women in the working class?

- Helen is described as a semi-whore. Discuss the depictions of women's lives and the poverty of the setting. According to late twentieth-century standards, would Helen still be described in this manner? Do you think that attitudes toward sexuality have changed that dramatically in the last forty years?

- Jo has some artistic talent and Geof is attending art school. Late in the play, the audience learns that Jo is able to earn some money touching up photos. Investigate the opportunities for aspiring artists. What kinds of jobs are available and how difficult is it to earn a living?

For her part, Helen has often hid the fact that she even has has a daughter, perhaps in the hopes of creating an illusion of youth for herself. Jo is abandoned by her mother whenever a better opportunity—usually a man with money—comes along. It is clear from her behavior that Jo desperately needs a mother. In the terms of a nurturing parent, Geof is the closest thing Jo has.

Pride

Jo has so much pride that she will not leave her flat once her pregnancy becomes evident. She certainly must be aware that she is the object of neighborhood gossip, but Jo refuses to face or acknowledge this negative attention. Staying a prisoner in her flat means that she cannot work, and so, she has no way to earn money and support herself. Pride is also an element of Helen's character: she is willing to push her illegitimate grandchild in a pram down neighborhood streets but when she discovers that the child is black, has too much pride to be seen with this particular child. Jo's pregnancy by a black man is not really a racial issue, rather it is a class issue. Jo and Helen may be poor, working class people, but Helen considers the black father to be from a class below their working class status. As such, Helen rejects Jo's unborn child, even offering to drown it or give it away, rather than be seen with it. Helen's misplaced pride permitted her to remain in a relationship with a man who mocked, humiliated, and eventually threw her out of his home, but this same pride causes her to reject her own grandchild, who is not deemed suitable.

The kind of pride exhibited in *A Taste of Honey* is not the positive kind that enables a character to rise above adversity. Rather, the misplaced dignity that Jo and Helen exhibit serves to chain them to their cycle of misery. They are too blinded by their skewed standards to break free of the confines of their existence.

Style

Angry Young Men

"Angry Young Men" was the label given to a group of British writers—notably playwright John Osborne—of the late-1950s, whose work expressed bitterness and disillusionment with Postwar English society. A common feature of their work is the antihero, a flawed, often abrasive character who rebels against a corrupt social order and strives for personal integrity. Delaney did not set out to become a part of this group, but when her play was produced, many critics saw her work as a protest against working class poverty and the hopelessness of a social system that confined people by status or class.

There are elements of the "Angry Theatre" in Delaney's play, notably its working class setting. But her characters are ultimately unmotivated. There is no sense that either Jo, Helen, or even Geof has an agenda to change the world, to correct the injustices of their existence. Unlike Jimmy Porter in Osborne's *Look Back in Anger*, Delaney's characters let life pass them by without attempting change, without lashing out, rebelling at their unfavorable situations. As Delaney frequently stated, however, her intention was to illuminate the working class in her play, to strive for realism. She was not angling for inclusion in the Angry Theatre.

Audience

The people for whom a drama is performed. Authors usually write with an audience in mind; however, Delaney is said to have written for actors, whom she felt were being given little enough to do in contemporary productions. One interesting aspect of *A Taste of Honey* is that Delaney frequently has her characters address the audience directly. In this sense she enables the actors to more fully realize their characterizations—engage in a kind of faux dialogue with "real" people (the audience). The technique also allowed the original audiences, many of whom had little contact with the social strata depicted in the play, a closer interaction with the working class.

Character

A person in a dramatic work. The actions of each character are what constitute the story. Character can also include the idea of a particular individual's morality. Characters can range from simple stereotypical figures to more complex multi-faceted ones. Characters may also be defined by personality traits, such as the rogue or the damsel in distress. "Characterization" is the process of creating a lifelike person from an author's imagination. To accomplish this the author provides the character with personality traits that help define who he will be and how he will behave in a given situation.

Genre

Genres are a way of categorizing literature. Genre is a French term that means "kind" or "type." Genre can refer to both the category of literature such as tragedy, comedy, epic, poetry, or pastoral. It can also include modern forms of literature such as drama novels or short stories. This term can also refer to types of literature such as mystery, science fiction, comedy, or romance. *A Taste of Honey* is generally classified as a realist, modern drama.

Plot

This term refers to the pattern of events. Generally plots should have a beginning, a middle, and a conclusion, but they may also sometimes be a series of episodes that are thematically linked (a technique frequently employed by German playwright Bertolt Brecht). Basically, the plot provides the author with the means to explore primary themes. The plot of *A Taste of Honey* is how Jo comes learns to live with her mother's abandonment, while finding the strength to survive. The theme of the play is the nature of the mother/daughter relationship.

Setting

The time, place, and culture in which the action of the play takes place is called the setting. The elements of setting may include geographic location, physical or mental environments, prevailing cultural attitudes, or the historical time in which the action takes place. The setting for *A Taste of Honey* is a run-down flat in a poor neighborhood. The action occurs over a nine to ten month period, roughly the gestation period for Jo's child.

Historical Context

England in the mid-to late-1950s was still feeling the effects of World War II. The bombing of London—the "Blitz" as it was often called—began September 7, 1940, and continued throughout the war. Children were sent out into the countryside for safety, and women in their twenties became eligible for the draft. Rationing of food, fuel, and other essentials needed for the war was common place. By 1944, Germany's secret weapon, the V2 ballistic missile began targeting London, intensifying the damage from years of earlier bombing. When the war ended, American soldiers returned home to a country that had suffered little damage within its borders.

Britain, on the other hand, had suffered greatly during the war and rebuilding would take a very long time. Rationing continued long after the end of the war. People needed homes as well as buildings in which to work and pray and, once again, enjoy life. The rebuilding of Britain's less tangible assets would take a long time, also. The war had intensified feelings about loyalty and betrayal, innocence and corruption, commitment and abandonment. The results of the Blitz and the images of the Holocaust had horrified Britains, but their endurance and survival had also strengthened the British resolve to reclaim their lifestyle.

In America, the suffering brought about by the

Great Depression and World War II ended in the Postwar boom of the 1950s. With the exception of minorities, notably black Americans, the 1950s were economically successful. But this was not the case in England, where huge numbers of the population were on relief, the British government's form of welfare. There was great despair over the future and society seemed brutal and mechanistic. This was especially true of the country's industrial heartland. One response to this feeling of despair was evident in the literature of the late-1950s. A group of young writers from this period were labeled "Angry Young Men" because their writings were filled with protest, bitterness, and anger at the social values that still prevailed in Britain.

Authors such as John Osborne, Kingsley Amis (*Lucky Jim* [1954]), Alan Sillitoe *(Loneliness of the Long Distance Runner* [1960]), and John Braine *(Room at the Top* [1957]) created the antihero as the protagonist of their works. These antiheroes were young people who could see that the upper classes had no desire to share the wealth or a willingness to help the lower classes achieve success. Osborne, and writers like him, viewed the upper classes and the institutions they had established with disdain. Delaney was hailed as a member of this group when *A Taste of Honey* was produced, although she was less concerned with social change than in creating realistic characters.

For the first time, the working class was finding a voice in England's literary works. These writers were not hailing from Britain's upper classes or from the genteel South. This new breed of writer understood the working class and asked "what is real?" Their response was that for the majority of Britains, poverty, dead-end jobs, and basic survival were "real." While life for the upper classes quickly returned to normal in the Postwar years, life for the workers did not improve; England, as a victorious nation, should have prospered across its classes, yet only a small minority were benefitting during this period.

English laborers could look to America and see that the middle class were prospering, pursuing the "American Dream." Jobs were plentiful and wages were increasing. Workers were buying automobiles and homes and the furniture to fill them. But in England, there was little hope for the future unless the working class could find a voice. The dramas and novels of protest advocating social changes offered working class Britains a voice. Despite Delaney's protestations that she was not a member of the Angry Theatre, her play nonetheless raised awareness of the plight of the lower classes.

Compare & Contrast

- **1958:** An English Roman Catholic economist, Colin Clark, condemns birth control. Clark argues that although population growth places difficult demands on agrarian societies, it also provokes greater efforts in the fields of industry, commerce, political leadership, and science.

Today: Birth control continues to be a politically charged issue, with murders, bombings, and increasing violence emerging as an increasingly frequent image in protests against abortion.

- **1958:** Agatha Christie's *Mousetrap* is the longest running play in British history, with over 2000 performances. Terrance Rattigan's *Variations on a Theme*, which opened on May 8, is credited as the play whose lack of content inspired Delaney to write *A Taste of Honey*.

  Today: Both *Mousetrap* and *A Taste of Honey* continue to be produced in regional theatre, but *Variations on a Theme* has achieved no lasting notoriety.

- **1958:** The Clean Air Act, passed in 1956, goes into effect. It represents Britain's efforts to cut down on deaths in London and in England's industrial cities, where many deaths are thought to be caused by the polluted air from factories and coal-burning furnaces.

  Today: Automobiles still cause pollution, but contamination from the burning of coal is significantly diminished. Britain continues its cleaning of public buildings, which for many years have been covered in the black soot left by burning coal.

- **1958:** For the first time, the British government allows women to sit in the House of Lords.

  Today: With a woman, Margaret Thatcher, having served several years as Prime Minister, women in Britain's Parliament are no longer considered novel or unusual.

Critical Overview

When *A Taste of Honey* opened on Broadway in October, 1960, most critics seemed more taken with the author's age than with her play. Almost every review commented upon Delaney's age, and a few upon her six foot height, but few endorsed the rousing success that the British critics bestowed upon the play. Most New York critics, instead, praised the cast and director, offering mixed praise for the play's content. These critics took a wait and see attitude toward Delaney's future prospects as a successful playwright.

In his review of *A Taste of Honey*, the *New York Time's* Howard Taubman stated that the play was "an evocation of disenchantment done with touching honesty." Taubman cited the play's honesty and "plainness of truth" as strengths of the writer, whom, he stated has a way of telling a story that is "modest, almost muted." Much of Taubman's praise, however, was directed toward the performers, especially Joan Plowright as Jo, who the critic felt "captures the shell of cynicism that the girl has grown to shield herself from her hopelessness."

Plowright provided a performance that Taubman called, "haunting." Of the playwright, Taubman noted that "the Lancashire lass may grow more optimistic as she grows older." Taubman, however, did not see Delaney's pessimism as a deterrent, finding in her play, "the redeeming savor of truth."

John McClain, writing for the *American Journal*, also found the honesty of the characters an important element of the play. McClain stated that Delaney "has not written a drama of any great significance, but she has a beautiful ear for dialogue and an amazingly uncluttered feeling for the people with whom she has grown up in her little Lancashire town." Delaney's ability to bring truth to her characters' voices is a strength, although that does not entirely make up for the lack of purpose in her play, according to McClain. Although Delaney's work lacks a political or sociological agenda, McClain pointed out that the play "is written with such obvious sincerity and familiarity, and it is so well played, that it becomes a very touching experience in the theatre." As did other reviewers, McClain also admired Plowright's performance as a highlight of the play.

Richard Watts Jr. also offered a strong endorsement in his review for the *New York Post*. Of the characters, Watts stated that they "have a warmblooded reality about them which reveals the young authoress as a dramatist who knows how to fill a play with recognizable and vivid human beings." Of the playwright, Watts praised Delaney and stating that "she knows how to create characters throbbing with life, she can build a dramatic situation with honesty and expertness, she writes a simple but vigorous prose and she has a compassion that is wry, unsentimental and always believable.

Without sacrificing her status as a realist, she can bring fresh imagination to the drabness of her narrative. Her drama has perhaps its weaker moments, but it rarely ceases to be effective." Watts's enthusiasm for Delaney, having referred to her as exhibiting "compassionate candor . . . [and] frank and explicit realism," was also extended to Plowright's performance, which he calls, "deeply moving."

Plowright was also a major strength of the play, according to the *New York World Telegram's* Frank Aston, who said that Plowright's is a "bravura" performance. Once again, as did other reviewers, Aston cited Delaney's honesty and reality in creating these characters and dialogue. But in the end, it was Plowright's skill as an actor that carried the show, providing "a moving experience."

Some reviewers offered a more mixed assessment of Delaney's play, including Walter Kerr of the *New York Herald Tribune*. Kerr disputed the realism of Delaney's dialogue, saying that "her people talk most strangely . . . they rap out words and phrases that now and then suggest they've all been given an aborted college education." But Kerr did think that Delaney created interesting characters, of whom all "pretensions to dignity" have been removed. *A Taste of Honey*, according to Kerr, "doesn't taste like honey, it tastes like vinegar spiced with ginger."

A less favorable review was provided by John Chapman in the *Daily News*. Chapman began by noting that Delaney's play made news in the

London theatrical world, that the young playwright was hailed as "a fresh, forceful new talent." But Chapman disagreed with this assessment. While he felt that Delaney "has a fine ability for creating believable characters [and] good skill at keeping them alive," the critic ultimately complained that her play is without any real purpose. Clearly disappointed that Delaney did not live up to her advance notices, Chapman complained that he "could not become emotionally involved in it [the play]."

Robert Coleman of the *New York Mirror* had similar reactions to Delaney's work. Coleman also observed that a playwright should have "something important to say." In a review that actually called Delaney names, Coleman referred to her as "a snarling, cynical young Englishwoman" who wrote "an ode to misery."

Slightly twenty years later, *A Taste of Honey* enjoyed a major revival, first appearing Off-Broadway and a few months later, on Broadway. Once again, the reviews were very mixed. In the *New York Times*, Frank Rich offered a mostly favorable review, saying of Delaney's play that "it holds up better than most plays of England's look-back-in-anger period." Rich complimented Delaney, saying "she looks at a miserable world with charity and humor." However, Rich's greatest kudos went to Amanda Plummer as Jo. Similar to the play's earlier production, it was the actress playing Jo who captured the hearts and imaginations of the reviewers.

John Beaufort provided a positive review in the *Christian Science Monitor*. Beaufort praised the honesty of Delaney's play, calling it "no nonsense realism, and deeply genuine compassion." But a less favorable criticism was offered by the *Daily News's* Douglas Watt, who said "the flavor's just about gone" on this twenty-year old play, which "hasn't worn very well." Watt argued that "the crudeness and contrived cheekiness of the dialogue stand out awkwardly, and the overall craftsmanship is negligible."

Within a few months of its Off-Broadway opening, Delaney's play moved to Broadway, where once again the critics were divided on the play's merits. In *Time*, T. E. Kalem called *A Taste of Honey* "taunt, vital, moving and funny." He reserved his greatest admiration for Plummer, however, saying that she "invests [Jo] with an unfaltering pulse beat of humanity" Jack Kroll of *Newsweek*, also found Plummer "unforgettable" in a performance that is "the making of an actress."

Plummer also received the only compliments to be found in Clive Barnes's review in the *New York Post*. Barnes, who found Delaney's play a bore, did find Plummer "radiant." Barnes's opinion of the 1981 revival was that "the boredom has intensified." Despite such mixed criticism, many have opined that credit must be given to Delaney for creating such a vivid protagonist. These critics argue that without the playwright's creative skills, actresses such as Plowright and Plummer would not continue to be singled out for praise.

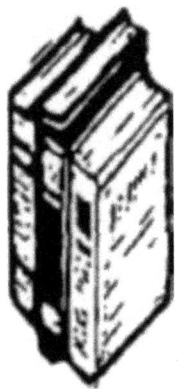

What Do I Read Next?

- Tillie Olsen's "I Stand Here Ironing" (1961) is a short story about the relationship between mother and daughter and the effects that poverty and a working class life can have on two people.

- *Saturday Night and Sunday Morning*, by Alan Sillitoe, is a novel about Britain's working class life.

- John Osborne's *Look Back in Anger* (1957) is a play that offers an antihero, Jimmy Porter, on the verge of the middle class but aware that the upper class can squash his climb up at any moment.

- Carolyn Kay Steedman's *Landscape for a Good Woman: A Story* (1987) is about growing up working class in

England and the struggle for survival.

- D. H. Lawrence's *Sons and Lovers* (1913) is set in the factory town of Nottinghamshire, a coal mining village. This novel is considered one of the first British novels to focus on working class life.

Sources

Aston, Frank. Review of *A Taste of Honey* in the *New York World Telegram*, October 5, 1960.

Barnes, Clive. Review of *A Taste of Honey* in the *New York Post*, May 6, 1981.

Beaufort, John. Review of *A Taste of Honey* in the *Christian Science Monitor*, May 6, 1981.

Boles, William. "'Have I Ever Laid Claims to Being a Proper Mother?' The Stigma of Maternity in Shelagh Delaney's *A Taste of Honey*" in *Text and Presentation*, Vol. 17, 1996, pp. 1-5.

Chapman, John. Review of *A Taste of Honey* in the *Daily News*, October 5, 1960.

Coleman, Robert. Review of *A Taste of Honey* in the *New York Mirror*, October 5, 1960.

Kalem, T. E. Review of *A Taste of Honey* in *Time*, July 6, 1982.

Kerr, Walter. Review of *A Taste of Honey* in the *New York Herald Tribune*, October 5, 1960.

Kroll, Jack. Review of *A Taste of Honey* in *Newsweek*, July 20, 1981.

McClain, John. Review of *A Taste of Honey* in the *New York Journal American*, October 5, 1960.

Rich, Frank. Review of *A Taste of Honey* in the *New York Times*, April 29, 1981.

Taubman, Howard. "Theatre without Illusion" in the *New York Times*, October 5, 1960.

Taylor, John Russell. "Way Down East: Shelagh Delaney" in *The Angry Theatre: New British Drama*, revised edition, Hill and Wang, 1969, pp. 117-40.

Watt, Douglas. Review of *A Taste of Honey* in the *Daily News*, April 29, 1981.

Watts Jr., Richard. Review of *A Taste of Honey* in the *New York Post*, October 5, 1960.

Whitehead, Susan. "Shelagh Delaney" in *Concise Dictionary of British Literary Biography*, Vol. 7: *Writers after World War II, 1945-1960*, Gale, 1991.

Further Reading

Campbell, Louise. *Coventry Cathedral: Art and Architecture in Postwar Britain*, Clarendon Press, 1996.

> While this book focuses on only one building, its construction represents many of the important Postwar ideas and forces found in architectural building in the 1950s and 1960s in England and Europe.

Ellis, Peter Berresford. *A History of the Irish Working Class*, by Pluto Press, 1996.

> This book provides an examination of the how the working class in Ireland has been shaped by economic, political, and social factors.

Jones, Gareth Stedman *Language of Class*, Cambridge University Press, 1984.

> This book is a collection of essays by a British social historian that discusses the nature of class consciousness and central issues of Britain's working class.

Taylor, John Russell. *The Angry Theatre: New British Drama*, Hill and Wang, 1969.

> This book provides biographies of

playwrights and a discussion of their individual works.

Throop, Elizabeth A. *Net Curtains and Closed doors: Intimacy, Family, and Public Life in Dublin*, Bergin & Garvey, 1999.

> This book focuses on the family life and the influences of religion, society, English Colonialism.